# EYE LEVEL IS BUY LEVEL:

The Power and Success of a Dope Tablescape

By:

Nichole Burton

ISBN: 978-1-7336439-9-3

Kincs by Nicki LLC
Website: https://www.kincsbynicki.com/

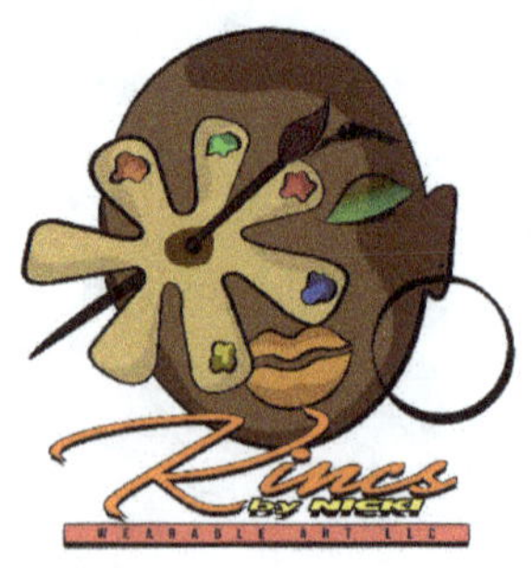

# Dedication:

For all upcoming and new-to-vending entrepreneurs, solopreneurs and MLM representatives.

For all the dope individuals who paved the way for all of us!!

# Acknowledgements:

For my children Jerald, Jade, Jalyn
and my buddy, Jax!

For Tika Lee who pushed me and
held me accountable!

# Table of Contents

# Introduction:

This guide was necessary... PERIOD! It was created to help business owners succeed at vending events and pop-up shops. We all know success equates to coins, but you must bring something to the table, literally, to draw customers in to spend their coins.

"I did then what I knew how to do. Now that I know better, I do better." – Maya Angelou

As a vendor, answer these questions:

Why do you struggle with securing the bag while vending?

Have you ever set up at a vendor event and wondered why your table gets bypassed by customers?

Did you prepare the layout of your table in advance?

How do you want potential clients/customers to remember you/your brand?

As an MLM consultant, how do you stand out from the rest?

Having a dope tablescape or display will attract people to your space, but creating the proper tablescape for events requires proper preparation. The goal is to have customers and potential clients leave your space feeling welcomed, and appreciative of the aesthetics of the space. The aesthetics will have them ready to help you secure the bag, which is one of the goals to setting up at a vendor event.

## *My Story*

I began my journey of aesthetically pleasing spaces while working in retail. For more than 30 years, I have loved executing floor sets. Customers often commented on my displays saying "You should consider your vendor space as that - a floorset which is a blueprint of the way you're going to design your space be it your home office, studio, or vending area. Being able to draw people visually is the key to helping them make a purchase, hence, securing the bag. My current journey is assisting my fellow vendors in presenting their best selves to the world of retail.

The goal of this guide is to help you create a dope tablescape, set-up or display. You will learn:

* how to ask the appropriate questions before choosing a sales opportunity

* how to prepare for your vending event

* time management

* and… Well, you'll have to finish the guide to get the 411!

Always remember- EYE LEVEL IS BUY LEVEL!!!

Chapter One:
# In the Beginning

## *Vendor License*

Some things should go without saying, but some people literally don't know what is required to even participate in vending events. Event hosts may require that you have your vendor's license prior to set-up at their public/city events. It is my opinion that they want to ensure that your business is just that - A BUSINESS. They want to assure that you are serious about vending your product and may determine that by your prior registration with your state agency. If you do not have your vendor or resell license (it could be called either based on the state that you registered), you can get registered by going to your state's Department of Taxation website. You can also find a list of the various types of vending licenses on the website as well.

### Accepting Payments

You do know that people still pay with cash, correct? Yes! Some customers prefer to pay with cash money. So, do you have the appropriate change for them if needed? When I am vending, I generally have between $80 - $100 in small dollar bills with me, carried in a money bag to create change for cash transactions. Not having cash on hand may result in missed sales. You can't fumble the bag like that! That's not dope!

Currently, I accept credit card payments through PayPal and Square. CashApp is fine to use with family and friends, but I do not recommend using it as a payment method for business. Particularly if you are planning to be in business long-term. Keep your Square and PayPal card readers with your ink pens, safety pins, and clothing tags, etc. The bag allows me to stay organized and have everything readily available in a pinch. Square and PayPal card readers are both free. Order them prior to your vendor events to be ready!

## Sales Tax

Now that you have obtained the appropriate license, collecting sales tax will be necessary because you have to report taxable income to your state's Department of Taxation monthly, quarterly, or bi-annually. The best way to handle this is to set up the tax percentage within the apps that you use to accept payments. As an added note, please be sure to stay on top of the current tax rate in your area and update as needed. Most states offer a few tax-free weekends on purchases of $75 or more. So, mark your calendars accordingly and apply this change when applicable.

### *Story time:*

Imagine you've done all the prep work for a three-day weekend vending experience. You're feeling good about yourself. For me, this was right on the cusp of the time of being able to take credit card payments in addition to accepting cash. We arrive at the venue Friday evening, get off the bus, gather our bags and head to our tables to begin setting up. I was pumped because it was the first time that I had a design printed and copy written, and I had a bunch available for purchase. Friday night went very well, and I was excited to see how the rest of the weekend would go.

Saturday morning, I went down to have breakfast and uncovered my table. I was open and ready for business before we had to go to the first session. Between the first and second sessions was lunch time which was also time for shopping. The resort venue also hosted other guests not attending our event. They saw that we had goods available and decided to shop as well.

A couple came to my table to select their items. I was excited and began bagging their goods. To pay for their order, they handed me their credit card, but I couldn't take it. I was a little upset, but the couple said that they would get cash and come back. The ATM was in the front of the resort and we were in the back. You guessed it; they didn't come back.

When we got back in town and I got settled and unpacked, the first thing I did was look into how to accept mobile credit card payments and I haven't looked back since.

I say all of this to say be mindful and try to cover all of your bases so that you don't lose any opportunities to make a sale.

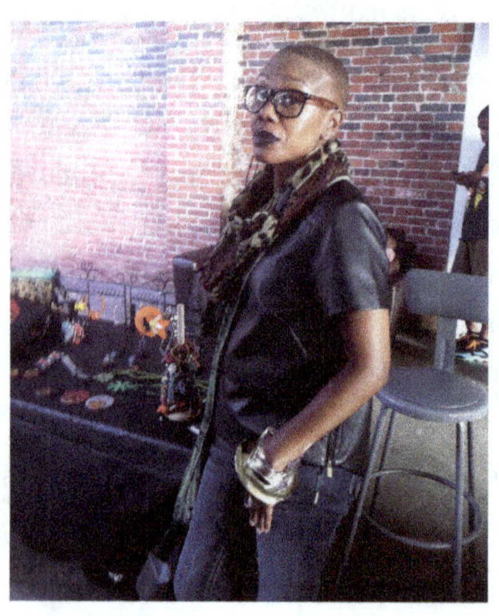

This tablescape occurred in 2012 at a fashion show. I began to think about my tablescape by adding a paper towel holder for my bracelets and 2 jewelry displays for my earrings and necklaces. I made sure my plastic tablecloth came as close to the ground as possible. In doing this I was able to hide my bag and suitcase from the public: which is how I carry my items into the venue.

## *Takeaways:*

Chapter Two:

# Preparation is Key

## *Venue Location*

It is imperative that you prepare for your route to the venue in advance. This may seem like a simple step, or maybe an unimportant one, but it can definitely make or break your day! I normally map out the trip process a week in advance. I do a drive by, if time allows, to check out the location of the venue. While there, I scan the area completely, look at the doors, parking area, everything. I track how long it'll take me to arrive on the day of the event. If I'm not able to physically get to the venue, I do a quick google search to check the surroundings. This is especially important if the event is out of town. You don't want any issues to arise that could've been prevented with a short prep session of the route.

## *Transporting Your Goods*

Oftentimes, we, as vendors, fail to think about how long it would take us to transport the goods into the venue for set up. A few other questions that we need answers to are: how early can you arrive for set up? Have you ever thought to count how many trips you have to make to your car to get all of your product inside? How close can you park to the entry of the building? Are there stairs or is there an elevator? Some of these questions can be answered by the event coordinator(s) before the day of the event. It is important to know the answers to these questions because it can affect your set-up time. I make no more than 4 trips to get all of my items inside. Once they're all in, I move my car so that I can focus solely on my tablescape.

## *Event Time Schedule*

Most venues will give a coordinator an hour to an hour and a half before the event set up time. The coordinator will usually open the doors at that time, which means they have a cut off time for setting up. It's very important to review your contract carefully for the events that you are registered because the contract gives pertinent details about the event. Arriving late and expecting extra accommodations is not only rude, but in some cases not permitted. If you arrive late, it's best to just go to your designated space and set up with the time remaining. If I know that my trips to and from the car take 20 minutes, I include that in my set-up time frame. You should get in the habit of tracking these types of things for every vending event, so that you can tweak your schedules as you see fit moving forward, improving what may need to be changed, etc.

## *Promoting the Event*

But hey! In all of your hustle and bustle, did you remember to promote the event that you are vending?

Oh, you didn't? Hmmmm... How do you think they're going to find you to purchase from you?  You're expecting someone ELSE to promote and share your brand? Shame on you!  You should've been pushing a flier through all of your social media pages, your personal page, text messages, emails, and all of your modes of communication.  You MUST promote your brand and the event that you are participating in as if it's your own. Your clients will show up for you, and even those who have never shopped with you before, may choose to come out to this particular event to see what you have to offer. They won't know that you're there without proper marketing. It's also a great idea to promote during the event. If sales are slow, or traffic is slow, post your items on social media and/or go live. This will pique people's interest, maybe urge them to drive to the event or possibly shop online, even if they can't be present. You can offer discounts to your clients that show up to the event. You could also have pre ordered items available to be picked up AT the event, to encourage customers to purchase something else. More often than not, they will buy a few more items or tell a friend about you. Get active and get creative!!

***Story time:***

I facilitated a paint party the night before a vending event the next morning. I really wanted to have all my items packed for both events but didn't have time or space. So, I got up super early the next morning, headed to my studio and unloaded the paint party items and loaded the vending items. As I finished up, it began to snow. Ugh… I didn't check the weather before leaving. However, I did check to see where I was going and knew the parking wasn't close the venue. Thank God, I left way earlier than I needed. The snow began falling harder and quickly. A 15-minute drive took me 35 minutes because of traffic. I finally arrive and pull up in a driveway close to the venue. Someone was there to assist me with the unloading of my car, thank God! But, I had to find parking and wasn't dressed appropriately for the weather. Boom! As I'm backing out of the driveway, a parking space opens up across the street from the venue. Woooo Hoooo! I was soaked and cold while setting up for the event but grateful that I had plenty of time to spare for my set-up and drying off. Remember preparation is key!!

## *Takeaways:*

---

---

---

---

---

---

---

---

---

---

---

Chapter Three:
# The Must Have's

I know that once you solidify your vending opportunity that you get excited, and just want to jump right in and get your items out to the world. That's great but, pause and take a breath. What does your brand represent? What do you want your ideal clientele to know about you? How will they be able to spot you in a room or space full of people?

Do you have a color scheme that represents your brand? How will it look when setting up for pop-up shops? Have you done a trial-run to see what that looks like? If not, why?

These are just a few things I want you to sit back and ponder on during your excitement. You can have a great product but featuring it on a less than stellar tablescape makes it unappealing. Let's fix that immediately!

**_A few pointers to get ya started are:_**

- Business cards: include name of your business, phone number, email address and website if available. If you have a logo, even better, add that too.

- Signage: This doesn't always have to be something ginormous. You can keep simple, yet effective, by placing your mission statement, images of your brand and/or pricing   sheets in frames to be placed on the table.

- Wear Your Brand - Whatever you are selling, t-shirts, jewelry, etc., this helps people visualize your products, see the quality, the fit, etc., it makes a differ-ence. You can also wear a company badge with your name, polo or dress shirt, or have customized products created that represent your brand such as t-shirts with your logo.

## *Tablecloths… to have or not to have?*

I know and understand that in the beginning it seems easy but creating a dope tablescape is more than just displaying your wares on a table with a tablecloth. You want to create a memorable experience for your customers and clientele. Your tablescape should be aesthetically pleasing. Your goal should be to present your best to the world, at all times, because you never know who is watching. Yes, you can throw some things on a table and hope for the best but, it'll cost you. It'll cost you time, sweat, blood, tears, and most importantly money.

Invest in your tablescape just as much as you invest in your product. Even if that means buying one piece at a time. Create a vision for your brand and start a tablescape budget. If you don't believe in your brand and set-up, no one else will. Start and invest now! This guide will help you do that (*see next chapter for detailed information about tablescape set-up*).

Most event spaces offer 6 ft rectangular or round tables for your set-up. Your tablecloth for the rectangular table should be 90"×132" long and 130" round for the round table. These lengths allow for you to hide all of your 'extras' under the table neatly-neatness matters!! Additionally, black tablecloths allow your items to pop. If you're a treats vendor, think about how an event planner might set up their treat table... Sparkly tablecloth with pretty sweets display fixtures.

**Story time:**

I own an insane number of tees, jewelry and sweatshirts from my business friends. I also love to wear them while vending. Bad move!

I was vending in February and as I got dressed, I decided to throw on a sweatshirt and earrings from one of my friends and proceed on with my day. I arrived at the event, set-up and relaxed for a few minutes before the people arrived. As they began to approach my table, I stood up, greeted them and began selling. One lady exclaims, "I love your sweatshirt, do you have anymore"? "No. My friend sells this sweatshirt", I replied. The lady asked, "Is she here?" I answered, "No, she isn't". The lady purchased a few items from me and as she walked away said, "I would've bought that sweatshirt too, if you had it". Now, I only rock my own brand while I'm vending or hosting a pop-up shop.

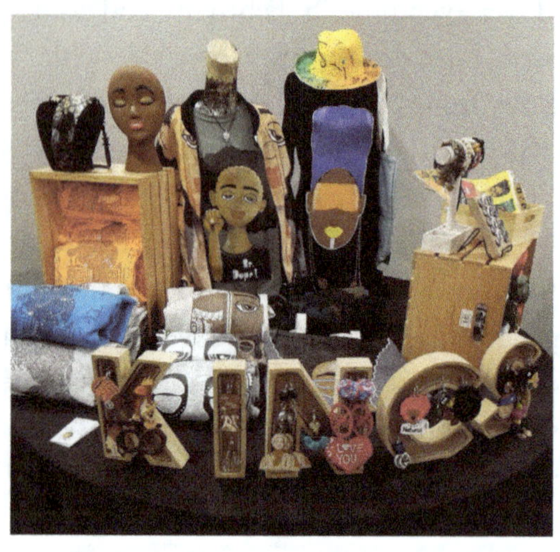

I found out the day before the event that I would have a round table in my space so I had to rearrange my vision for my tablescape. I bought the letters from Michael's one at a time until I had all five letters. The letters double as branding awareness and an earring holders, which was a dope investment. Due to spacing restrictions, I used mannequins to display my dress and jackets. The space on top of the crates can be used to hold additional display fixtures.

## *Takeaways:*

# Chapter Four

# The Set-Up

## *Stand Out*

Wwhat makes your brand stand out, is up to you. Your tablescape is your way of saying, here I am. Dope set-ups and tablescape's are being watched by event planners and big brands. Big box brands have a social media team that pays attention to what's being posted on social media. Presentation is key!! Some of the benefits of investing in your tablescape are:

- brand awareness,
- gain a following on social media,
- being recruited for high-end or national events.

Elevating items from "flat on the table" displays to "EYE LEVEL IS BUY LEVEL" displays is strictly centered around your fixtures. Fixtures can be but not limited to:

- crates (small, large)
- plastic shelving units
- peg boards
- bracelet holders
- easels
- frames
- mannequins

Leveling up your tablescape means building the infrastructure of your table. Think of yourself as an architect! Let's use crates as an example: I use crates to not only carry in my t-shirts or other items into the vending event, I also use them to display my goods on the table. Crates can be used in many ways, they can be displayed horizontally and vertically depending on your design, can be used to put items into, or turned upside down and used as a sort of table or shelf. Extra-large plastic clips can be used to hold the crates together to ensure security of your set-up. You can have wood cut and used as shelves in your crates and these units can be used for a candle company, body or hair products. Cup hooks can be screwed into your crates on the inside or outside to create a jewelry display.

If you sell jewelry, such as earrings or necklaces, peg boards on an easel can be utilized for a dope display. You can sort them from the shortest to longest, posts or dangles or colors. Remember, you want your merch to '**POP**' while displayed. Leaving your fixtures, in their natural state, adds character and a visually dope background for your colorful items. You can use a wire mannequin bust to also display your earrings or what makes sense for your brand. If you have multiples of the same earrings, put out a few pairs and put the others away. TAKE YOUR EARRINGS OUT OF THE PLASTIC and don't lay them flat on the table. These are easy items for people to potentially grab and go without paying. You don't want anyone taking advantage of you and getting free product! Having a mirror available for your customers to check themselves out in your products is a great addition to your tablescape as well.

Plastic shelving is another fixture that's easy to carry in and set-up. You can use them on or off of the table. They can be set up as 1 whole fixture or 2 separate units.

Bracelets can be displayed on 1-, 2- or 3- tiered bracelet stands. If you get the black velvet stands, make sure you have a lint roller for appearance purposes. Try to catch them on sale to save a few coins, but they are definitely a great investment if you sell jewelry. If you are able to borrow some stands and other fixtures, do so! It's cool. Swallow your pride until you are able to purchase your own. Paper towel holders can be used as bracelet stands or you can make them with a dowel rod, wood circle, wood glue and a screw. GET CREATIVE!

Most vendor spaces are 10'×10' and will allow you to bring in fixtures as long as they fit in your space. Apparel such as jackets, dresses or pants can be displayed on a clothing rack, but again, make sure the rack fits in your allotted space and is collapsible; this makes set-up and break down easier. If you are using hangers, hang the apparel with the same color hangers, facing the same way and from shortest to longest or by color scheme, to make the look more cohesive.

Mannequins give your table an additional '**Pop**' by having your merch displayed. People can get an idea of how the item will fit them by seeing it displayed this way. Hat mannequins are great for toboggans, baseball and top hats and will give you additional space on your table. Mannequins can sit on top of your crates to displayed what's folded or your shelving unit. If it's a hanging mannequin, you'll need to have something heavy to sit in it to keep it from falling. If you have a clothing rack, hang the mannequin from there.

Folding is an important part of your

tablescape; it's bomb if you have retail experience but if not, you can use a piece of cardboard to help you fold your shirts. Display them from smallest to largest and know how many you have in each size.

If you provide paper products, i.e., cards, coloring books, etc., smaller crates are a great way to display them. By putting the paper products in a sleeve, it'll prevent them from getting smudges and dirty. The small crates allow additional space on your table for business cards and such.

Frames and easels provide a unique way to display your pricing lists, bio and images of your products. If you have a color scheme, purchase frames to match. Table and floor easels are useful in displaying artwork. STOP LAYING YOUR ART ON THE TABLE!!! Prints in a plastic sleeve can be displayed in a create or magazine rack with a price tag.

If you can find or build fixtures that represent your brand, go for it!

## *Invest in Yourself*

The goal to vending is to see a return on your investment, period! You should know where to set-up as a vendor and where your brand doesn't belong. This process will take time because in the beginning, you'll want to be everywhere. When event coordinators post fliers promoting their event on social media, that's not the time to ask if they're looking for vendors. Unless coordinators are specifically asking for vendors, you should plan to be in the next event.  Think about a time when you've seen a completed flier promoting an event that has ticket sales attached. Have you ever thought about why later on, that coordinator may be asking for vendors close to the event date? Think about it… You or your brand are not afterthoughts! You have permission to ask questions in regard to the vendor set-up.

Questions I've asked are:

- are you recreating the flier to include my logo?

- is the fee discounted due to your lack of planning?

If no is the answer to either, I'm unavailable and you should be also. Don't allow anyone to "pimp" your brand.

### *Story time:*

I was included in a messenger group looking for vendors for a comedy show. The show had a flier with all of the information and sponsors were listed. The people attending the show paid for tickets to see a comedy show and whatever else they offered. Do you think people would be wanting to shop with vendors? So, I asked if the flier be recreated to include logos and how will we be promoted. I was deleted from the group for asking questions. Anyone asking for your money should be able to answer any questions you have. I had other people from the group message me separately saying, I didn't think to ask those questions. Be careful and mindful about where and with whom you spend your money.

On another note, having a dope tablescape and set-up got me recruited to participate in the National Urban League conference, which is a high-end event. Do you believe in what you're presenting?

## *Tablescape Examples*

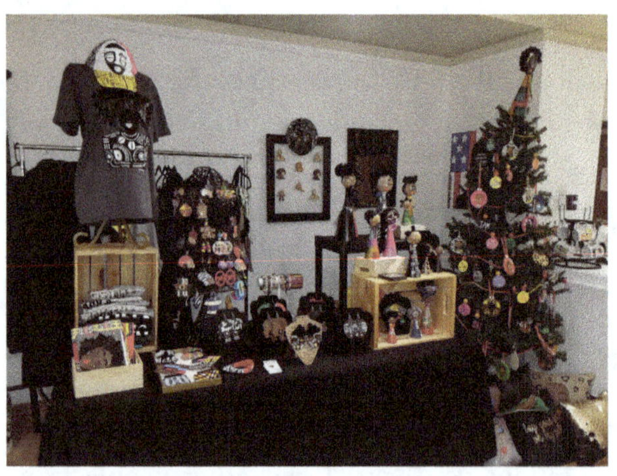

This type of set-up happens when vending over a 3 day period. Crates (small and large), along with plastic shelving and jewelry fixtures created the infrastructure for this tablescape. The space allotted me enough room for a clothing rack, wall space for artwork and a Christmas tree. Adding real props or accents to your space allows extra room on your table for more Merchandise. I brought in a rug to set underneath the tree which created a cozy display for the pillows.

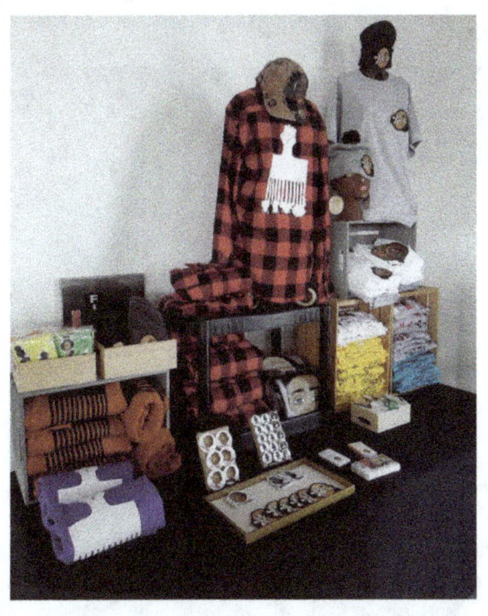

By using mannequins on top of the crates and plastic shelving unit, I was able to build my display upwards. The burlap canvases serve as a dope backdrop for my buttons. The holes in the burlap allow the pin to slide in easily and use wire easels to complete the look. The stickers and patches are sitting on a tray with a velvet board insert. The tray can also be used as a jewelry holder by pushing the earring hooks through the velvet or straight pins to display necklaces.

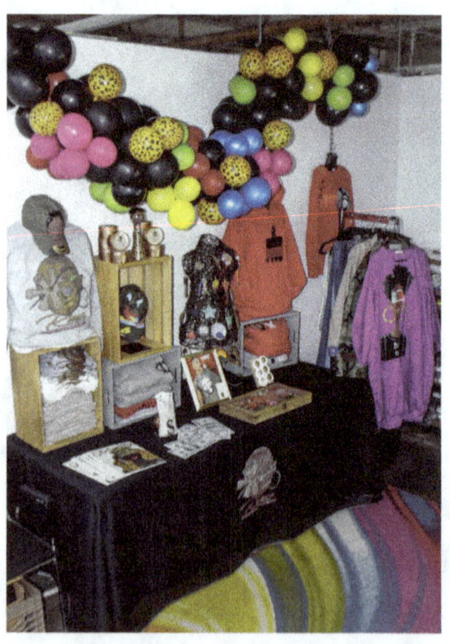

This tablescape resides in my studio where I stream my live shows for social media. I added a framed picture of myself wearing my product. Price lists can also be displayed this way. I partnered with Silver Confetti Balloon Boutique to enhance my space and tablescape. This look can be achieved while vending by taping them to your table. Dont be afraid to collaborate with another business while promoting your brand-as long as the brands blend cohesively. This collaboration can be win-win for all involved. I also had my logo added to my tablecloth.

## Takeaways:

# Chapter Five

# The Follow UP

---

## *PLAN YOUR WORK AND WORK YOUR PLAN!*

The event has come to an end, you've packed and headed home. Did you meet new people, potential customers and clients? How will you stay in touch with them? Giving business cards is great but you'll end up waiting on THEM to reach out to YOU. By having an email signup sheet strategically placed on your table, you'll be able to follow up about their experience at your table, send out sale notifications, etc. Anything that you'd like to convey to the potential customer you can do so if you gather their email address. You can place the sheets on a clip board, or even have a book with lined paper to gather the information. Again, people will always remember how you made them feel during their shopping experience. Go all out!

### *Story time:*

I have a long-time client who shops with me often. She isn't on social media, at all, so I call or text her to inform her about my events. If I call, we end up catching up and sharing deets about everyday life. She's always appreciative of me making sure I include her in my whereabouts. 9 times out of 10 when she shows up, she's rocking my brand.

Put effort into making others feel great about spending money with you.

You should journal your reflections from the event. Ask yourself the following questions:

- What went well?
- What didn't work?
- What could you change?

- What did you learn?
- Was it profitable? If not, why?
- If the event is offered again, would you attend? Why or why not?
- Does my brand belong here?

Your answers will assist you with booking future events, set-up and what *does* work. Reflect after every event you do.

## *Takeaways:*

_______________________________

_______________________________

_______________________________

_______________________________

_______________________________

_______________________________

_______________________________

_______________________________

_______________________________

_______________________________

_______________________________

_______________________________

# Chapter Six

# The Virtual Experience

### *The Virtual Shift*

Did you make a pivot in 2020? The virtual pivot is what I'm speaking of. If you did not create a virtual footprint for your brand during the beginning of the pandemic, what are you waiting for? Selling virtually will save you from paying vendor fees. You should not have to or need to pay a fee for a virtual selling experience. If you have a social media page or pages, you should be selling your merch. MLM representatives have paved the way for entrepreneurs in this venture, if you've been paying attention.

Create a space in your home, office or studio where you can set up a vendor table. You should still create the same dopeness virtually. It draws the crowd in. Once you have the items you want to present, create a list with a number and price for each item and set them up in order. Invest in a ring light, if you don't have one. The light illuminates your product when brought close to the light. Use the free site called Canva to create a digital flier and begin to market your showing a month in advance. Post teasers on social media and DO NOT RESPOND to the comments. The reason I suggest that you don't respond the comments is because it builds the anticipation. Push your flier each week until the day of selling.

Day of…get dressed, add a little lipstick or get a fresh haircut and go live!! Have a virtual assistant help you to collect the numbers and email addresses for invoicing. Be perky, fun and energetic while selling! It adds to the ambiance. You should have a sales goal before starting and push to reach it by the end of your showing. The goal is to sell out, PERIOD!!

At this point, you should be standing, and all items should be unwrapped and easily accessible. Standing up while showing allows you to grab the items and be able to hold them up to your person. Creating a visual of where items sit or lay, assists with sales. Allow your followers to come into the live before jumping into selling. Greet them, pin the rules in the comment section and reiterate them periodically throughout the live. Once you have a nice amount of people, begin selling. I would choose not to play music while on Facebook because they'll end up muting a part of your video later on down the line.

Happy sales! Follow up with your virtual assistant and send invoices. Give the customers a deadline on when they need to pay their invoices and pick up their items. Be stern and stick to your rules!!

Pivot, Aim, Shoot and Follow through!!

### *Story time:*

I scheduled my first live in 2020 and was a nervous wreck. I stayed up late painting merch and setting up my studio. The day came for the live and we were ready to go. The one thing I didn't think of was not to have the earrings in the background. Earrings are one of my biggest sellers and was what everybody was waiting for… I made them wait until the end. That live went very well but was a little chaotic on the back end for me. I had to watch the replay 3 times to ensure I had the correct information for invoicing.

That live taught me to always have a virtual assistant paying attention and writing the information down clearly. I now have a system that works and love selling virtually!!

## *Takeaways:*

Chapter Seven:
# And That's A Wrap

Yo! After implementing these tips, you should have secured the bag by leveling up!!! There is one thing you should remember about your tablescape; YOU CAN ALWAYS GO UP!!! Even if you're in the middle of a room, your tablescape should be seen as soon as people come through the door. The goal is to SECURE THE BAG, PERIOD!! Add elements of your brand to your table. If you crochet, add yarn and knitting needles as a part of your design. They'll want to buy it. You should set a sales goal and aspire to beat it while vending. Set yourself apart from the crowd by achieving a dope tablescape. Always remember that people love looking at and purchasing pretty things. Cheers to leveling up, literally, and securing the bag! Cha ching!!

I want to see you win at vending! You should be able to 'see' your design or set-up before you set up. MLM, you should stand out by being extra creative in your tablescape. Why should I buy from you? Keep this in the back of your mind while choosing your events.

**Story time:**

I saw one Paparazzi vendor at an event, and she didn't have anything pink. Her set-up and tablescape was impeccable!! Her motive was clear acrylic and unfinished wood which helped her accessories STAND OUT!! Her display was also not overwhelming, which is memorable. This is where you want to be!!

## *Takeaways:*

# Vendor Checklist:

- Marketing
- Merchandise
- Table (for backup)
- Tablecloths
- Fixtures
- Business cards
- Change (Bills and coins)
- Signage
- Bags (for purchases)
- Price list(s)
- Credit card swipers

# About the Author

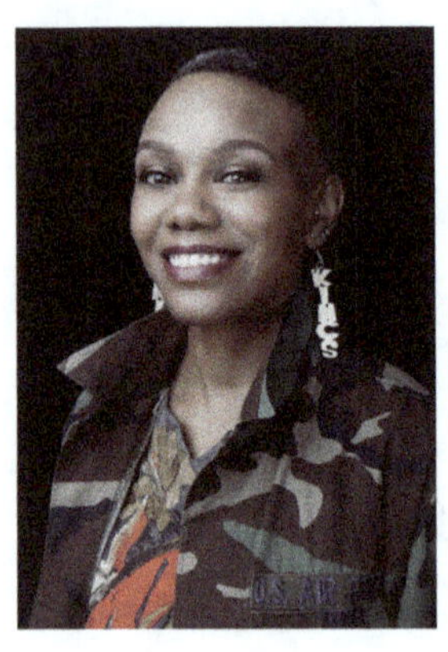

At the age of five, **Kincs by Nicki,** Founder and Designer Nichole "Nicki" Burton began her journey as an artist. A Columbus, Ohio native; Burton is a self-taught artist and designer who has turned her passion for drawing and painting into a sustainable enterprise. Burton's creative instinct propels her to experiment with color and texture, producing a signature style that has evolved into a vibrant brand of wearable art that is far from ordinary.

A classic **Kincs by Nicki** creation is

uniquely outstanding because Burton masterfully combines colors, textiles and cultural relevancy together to create pieces that resonate with its future owner. "Art should be appreciated; not discarded in a basement or lost in a jewelry box." Keeping with her belief that each piece should be a one-of-a-kind work of art, she intentionally ensures that no one, hand-painted piece is the same. "Everything I create is intentional and meaningful to the entire collection."

Burton's process for creating new pieces manifest in the forms of dreams. "No pencil or stencil. It is all in my head." It is no wonder that Nichole's statement-making jewelry and clothing reflects the city that she inhabits and works in which is bedecked in culturally significance and imaginative representation. Over the course of her successful 20+-year career, Nichole has collaborated with designers, photographers, stylists, make-up artists and activists to highlight, enlighten and educate the significance and relevancy of African American art.

Additionally, Nichole also operates a mobile art studio that turns any location into an art studio in minutes. She also hosts themed "Paint & Sip" events throughout the year.

She currently resides in Columbus, Ohio with her husband, three adult children and one grandchild.

# Additional Information

Do you want to grab my Free Swag Bag ideal list? Sign up and download the free list at

http://bit.ly/freeswagbaglist

Need help with setting up your events? Schedule a consulting appointment where I can help you virtually or in-person at

http://bit.ly/booknicki

Visit my website for uniquely handcrafted products, candles, sip and paint parties and much, much more at:

https://www.kincsbynicki.com/